Math

2

Grade 2

Play Ball

Find the answers. Then connect the dots. Start with 0.

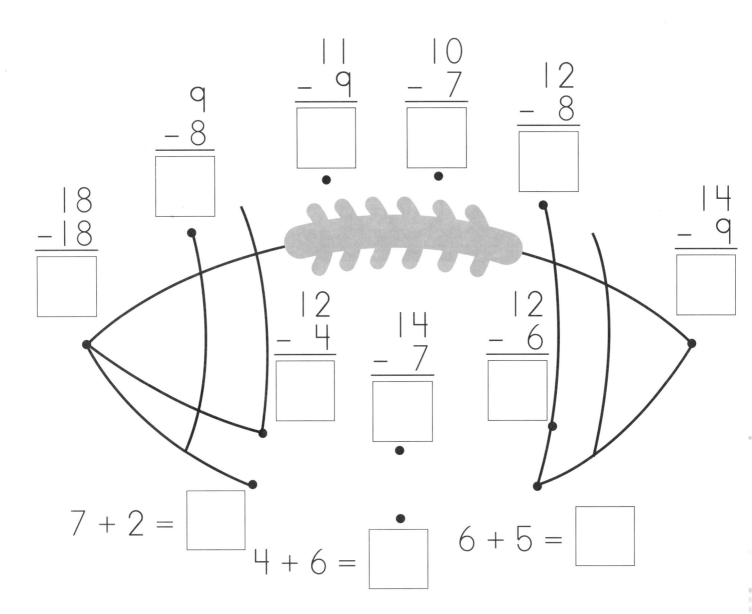

$$9 - 8 = \boxed{}$$

$$11 - 9 = \boxed{}$$

$$10 - 7 = \boxed{}$$

$$12 - 8 = \boxed{}$$

$$18 - 18 = \boxed{}$$

$$14 - 9 = \boxed{}$$

$$12 - 4 = \boxed{}$$

$$14 - 7 = \boxed{}$$

$$12 - 6 = \boxed{}$$

$$7 + 2 = \boxed{}$$

$$4 + 6 = \boxed{}$$

$$6 + 5 = \boxed{}$$

Circle the name of the ball you made.

baseball   football   golf ball

EMC 4176 • © Evan-Moor Corp.

Find the answers to help the bowling ball hit the pin.

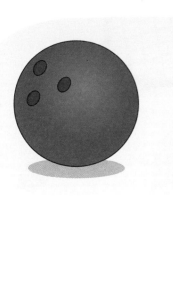

$$\begin{array}{r} 9 \\ + 7 \\ \hline \end{array}$$

$$\begin{array}{r} 7 \\ + 6 \\ \hline \end{array}$$

$$\begin{array}{r} 14 \\ - 5 \\ \hline \end{array}$$

$$\begin{array}{r} 8 \\ + 4 \\ \hline \end{array}$$

$$\begin{array}{r} 8 \\ + 7 \\ \hline \end{array}$$

$$\begin{array}{r} 15 \\ - 9 \\ \hline \end{array}$$

$$\begin{array}{r} 8 \\ + 8 \\ \hline \end{array}$$

$$\begin{array}{r} 17 \\ - 8 \\ \hline \end{array}$$

$$\begin{array}{r} 9 \\ + 6 \\ \hline \end{array}$$

$$\begin{array}{r} 8 \\ + 5 \\ \hline \end{array}$$

$$\begin{array}{r} 7 \\ + 3 \\ \hline \end{array}$$

$$\begin{array}{r} 18 \\ - 9 \\ \hline \end{array}$$

Tennis, Anyone?

 Find the answers.

$$45 + 13$$

$$14 + 23$$

$$23 + 74$$

$$56 + 32$$

$$35 + 52$$

$$20 + 20$$

$$62 + 14$$

$$77 + 21$$

$$55 + 14$$

$$14 + 41$$

$$88 + 10$$

EMC 4176 • © Evan-Moor Corp.

Take Me Out to the Ballgame

▶ Find the answers.

The larger number wins.
Circle the winner.

```
  54          33          75          86
 -21         -12         -52         -36
 ┌──┐        ┌──┐        ┌──┐        ┌──┐
 │33│        │21│        │  │        │  │
 └──┘        └──┘        └──┘        └──┘

  39          93          77          81
 -33         -42         -23         -60
 ┌──┐        ┌──┐        ┌──┐        ┌──┐
 │  │        │  │        │  │        │  │
 └──┘        └──┘        └──┘        └──┘

  76          65          89          84
 -21         -30         -67         -23
 ┌──┐        ┌──┐        ┌──┐        ┌──┐
 │  │        │  │        │  │        │  │
 └──┘        └──┘        └──┘        └──┘
```

Kisha's Favorite Ballgame

▶ Color each square where the answer has a **6** in the **tens** place.
This will tell you the first letter of Kisha's favorite ballgame.
Circle the picture of her favorite game.

85 −33	74 −12	89 −28	34 +33	47 −42
29 −19	35 +34	54 −21	88 −10	86 −36
23 +74	75 −11	85 −22	44 +25	76 −21
56 −32	77 +12	93 −42	45 +24	65 −30
20 +70	60 + 9	99 −34	40 +28	88 +10

EMC 4176 • © Evan-Moor Corp.

▶ Answer the subtraction problems.
Then add the numbers to see if you are correct.

```
 54      33
-21  X  +21
 33      54
```

```
 86      □
-34  X  +34
 □       □
```

```
 94      □
-42  X  +42
 □       □
```

```
 75      □
-44  X  +44
 □       □
```

```
 39      □
-27  X  +27
 □       □
```

```
 83      □
-50  X  +50
 □       □
```

```
 75      □
-34  X  +34
 □       □
```

```
 86      □
-33  X  +33
 □       □
```

```
 67      □
-42  X  +42
 □       □
```

Catch the Ball

▶ Match the balls and gloves.

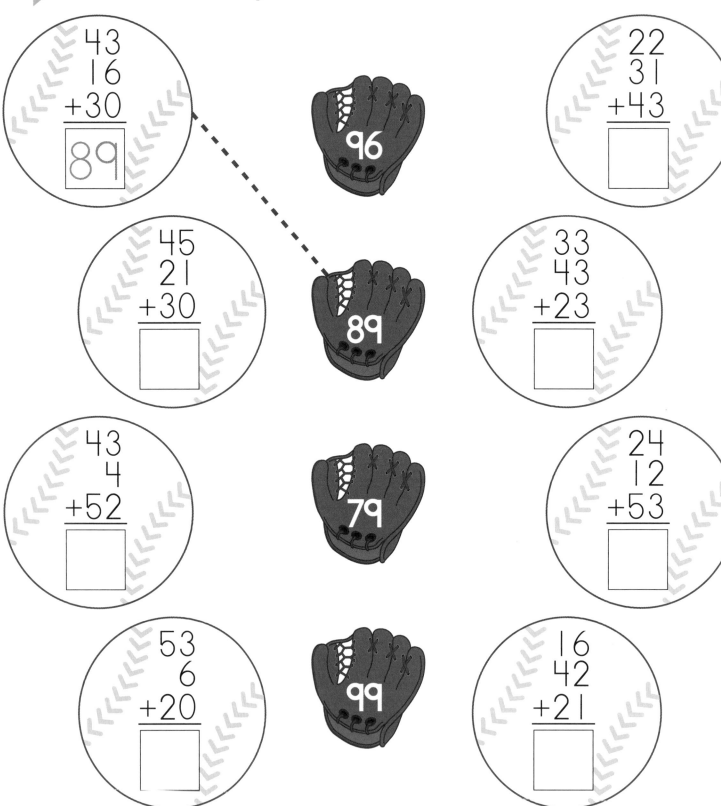

43
16
+30

89

22
31
+43

96

45
21
+30

33
43
+23

89

43
4
+52

79

24
12
+53

53
6
+20

99

16
42
+21

▶ Read. Write the problems. Answer them.

Matt's team played 28 games. They lost 13 games. How many games did they win?

Matt's team won 15 games.

```
  28
- 13
  15
```

Maria made 33 baskets. Molly made 46 baskets. How many baskets did they make in all?

The girls made ☐ baskets in all.

Mr. Brown's sports shop sold 23 football helmets on Saturday and 15 helmets on Monday. How many helmets did he sell?

Mr. Brown sold ☐ helmets in all.

What's for Dinner?

▶ After the basketball game the team went for dinner.
Use the code to find what the team ate.

Code

24 = P	33 = M	54 = Z	65 = A	78 = I
30 = N	39 = E	63 = L	70 = D	99 = O

```
  69    51    88    96    23          33    90    50
 -45   +27   -34   -42   +42         +32   -60   +20
┌───┐ ┌───┐ ┌───┐ ┌───┐ ┌───┐       ┌───┐ ┌───┐ ┌───┐
│24 │ │   │ │   │ │   │ │   │       │   │ │   │ │   │
└───┘ └───┘ └───┘ └───┘ └───┘       └───┘ └───┘ └───┘

  P    ___   ___   ___   ___         ___   ___   ___
```

```
  86    24    79    54    62    42    30    15
 -23   +15   -46   +45   -32   +23   +40   +24
┌───┐ ┌───┐ ┌───┐ ┌───┐ ┌───┐ ┌───┐ ┌───┐ ┌───┐
│   │ │   │ │   │ │   │ │   │ │   │ │   │ │   │
└───┘ └───┘ └───┘ └───┘ └───┘ └───┘ └───┘ └───┘

 ___   ___   ___   ___   ___   ___   ___   ___
```

Number Puzzle

Find the answers. Write the answers in the puzzle boxes.

Across

2.
$$43 \\ +22 \\ \overline{}$$
65

4.
$$96 \\ -60 \\ \overline{}$$

6.
$$52 \\ +33 \\ \overline{}$$

8.
$$70 \\ +21 \\ \overline{}$$

10.
$$14 \\ +61 \\ \overline{}$$

12.
$$79 \\ -33 \\ \overline{}$$

(Crossword grid)
1 — 2
2 — 6 3 — 5
4   5
6   7
8   9
10 11
12

Down

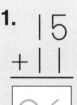

1.
$$15 \\ +11 \\ \overline{}$$
26

3.
$$96 \\ -43 \\ \overline{}$$

5.
$$34 \\ +34 \\ \overline{}$$

7.
$$89 \\ -30 \\ \overline{}$$

9.
$$59 \\ -42 \\ \overline{}$$

11.
$$42 \\ +12 \\ \overline{}$$

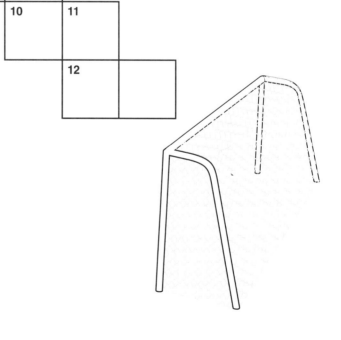

Regrouping

▶ Regroup to make **one more** set of ten.

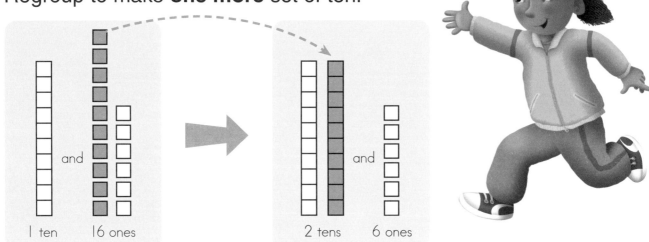

1 ten and 19 ones = __2__ tens and __9__ ones

3 tens and 12 ones = _____ tens and _____ ones

5 tens and 16 ones = _____ tens and _____ ones

▶ Regroup to make **one less** set of ten.

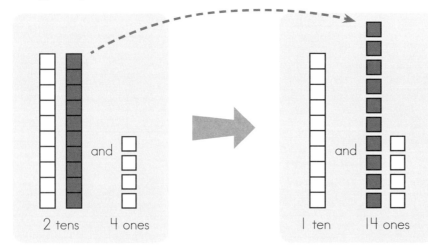

6 tens and 5 ones = _____ tens and _____ ones

9 tens and 2 ones = _____ tens and _____ ones

8 tens and 6 ones = _____ tens and _____ ones

Regrouping

▶ If the **ones** place adds up to more than **9**, you must **regroup**.
That means you move the **tens** to the **tens place**.

Here's how:

```
  16
+ 16
```
Add the ones.

```
1
  16
+ 16
   2
```
Write the ones.
Move the tens to
the tens place.

```
1
  16
+ 16
  32
```
Add the tens.

▶ Add. Regroup.

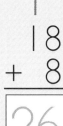

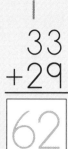

```
1
  18
+  8
  26
```

```
1
  33
+ 29
  62
```

```
  57
+ 18
```

```
  44
+ 28
```

```
  65
+ 15
```

```
  29
+ 29
```

```
  15
+ 68
```

```
  77
+ 13
```

```
  19
+ 47
```

```
  38
+ 38
```

Go for the Goal!

▶ Add to find the answers. Regroup when needed.
Color the football with the largest answer brown.

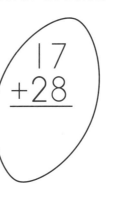

$$\begin{array}{r} 19 \\ +\ 5 \\ \hline 24 \end{array}$$

$$\begin{array}{r} 28 \\ +\ 6 \\ \hline \end{array}$$

$$\begin{array}{r} 17 \\ +28 \\ \hline \end{array}$$

$$\begin{array}{r} 36 \\ +14 \\ \hline \end{array}$$

$$\begin{array}{r} 54 \\ +14 \\ \hline \end{array}$$

$$\begin{array}{r} 19 \\ +19 \\ \hline \end{array}$$

$$\begin{array}{r} 67 \\ +24 \\ \hline \end{array}$$

$$\begin{array}{r} 29 \\ +16 \\ \hline \end{array}$$

$$\begin{array}{r} 10 \\ +17 \\ \hline \end{array}$$

$$\begin{array}{r} 25 \\ +45 \\ \hline \end{array}$$

$$\begin{array}{r} 38 \\ +32 \\ \hline \end{array}$$

$$\begin{array}{r} 25 \\ +38 \\ \hline \end{array}$$

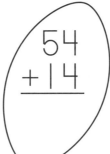

EMC 4176 • © Evan-Moor Corp.

Adding Three Numbers

Find the answers. Regroup if needed.

```
  48        26        73        25
  34        13         9        12
+ 42      + 31      + 16      + 31
┌─────┐   ┌─────┐   ┌─────┐   ┌─────┐
│ 124 │   │     │   │     │   │     │
└─────┘   └─────┘   └─────┘   └─────┘


  66        43        15        25
  25        12        31        15
+  8      + 50      + 21      + 35
┌─────┐   ┌─────┐   ┌─────┐   ┌─────┐
│     │   │     │   │     │   │     │
└─────┘   └─────┘   └─────┘   └─────┘


  16        50        23        13
  33        40        43        47
+ 28      + 30      + 13      + 21
┌─────┐   ┌─────┐   ┌─────┐   ┌─────┐
│     │   │     │   │     │   │     │
└─────┘   └─────┘   └─────┘   └─────┘
```

Regroup to Subtract

▶ If the **ones** place cannot be subtracted, you must **regroup**. This means you move a set of 10 to the **ones place**.

Here's how:

```
 2 10
 3̸0̸
+12
```
Regroup a ten to make more ones. Move the ones to the ones place.

```
 2 10
 3̸0̸
+12
  8
```
Subtract the ones.

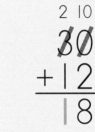

```
 2 10
 3̸0̸
+12
 18
```
Subtract the tens.

▶ Subtract. Regroup.

```
 2 14
 3̸4̸
-16
 18
```

```
 4 13
 5̸3̸
-38
 15
```

```
 55
-28
```

```
 55
-46
```

```
 70
-25
```

```
 95
-38
```

```
 74
-36
```

```
 88
-49
```

```
 41
-29
```

```
 66
-17
```

EMC 4176 • © Evan-Moor Corp.

▶ Draw lines to match the problems with their answers.
Regroup if needed.

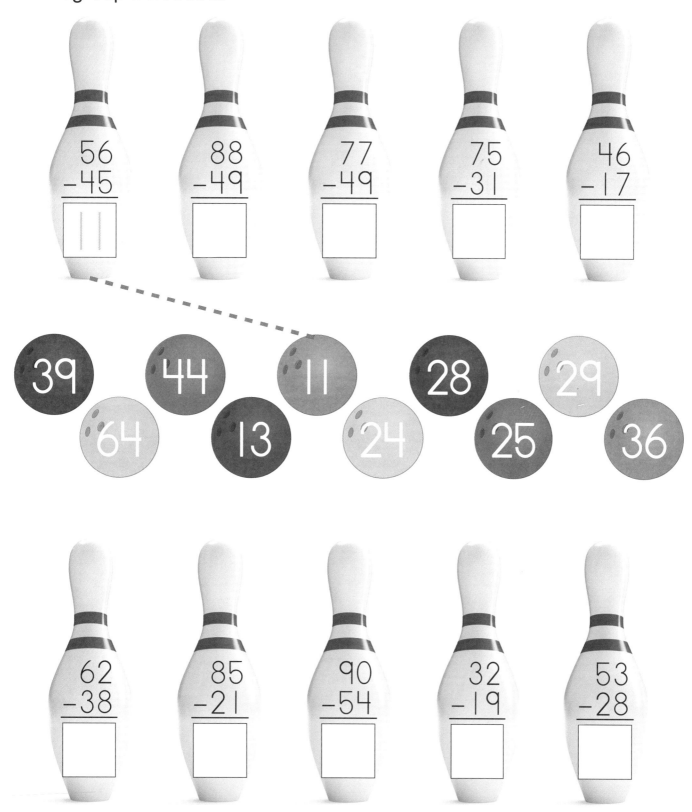

$$\begin{array}{r} 56 \\ -45 \\ \hline \end{array}$$

$$\begin{array}{r} 88 \\ -49 \\ \hline \end{array}$$

$$\begin{array}{r} 77 \\ -49 \\ \hline \end{array}$$

$$\begin{array}{r} 75 \\ -31 \\ \hline \end{array}$$

$$\begin{array}{r} 46 \\ -17 \\ \hline \end{array}$$

39   44   11   28   29
64   13   24   25   36

$$\begin{array}{r} 62 \\ -38 \\ \hline \end{array}$$

$$\begin{array}{r} 85 \\ -21 \\ \hline \end{array}$$

$$\begin{array}{r} 90 \\ -54 \\ \hline \end{array}$$

$$\begin{array}{r} 32 \\ -19 \\ \hline \end{array}$$

$$\begin{array}{r} 53 \\ -28 \\ \hline \end{array}$$

A Hole in One

Add or subtract. Regroup if needed. Then draw a line through the problems that equal **53** to get the golf ball into the hole.

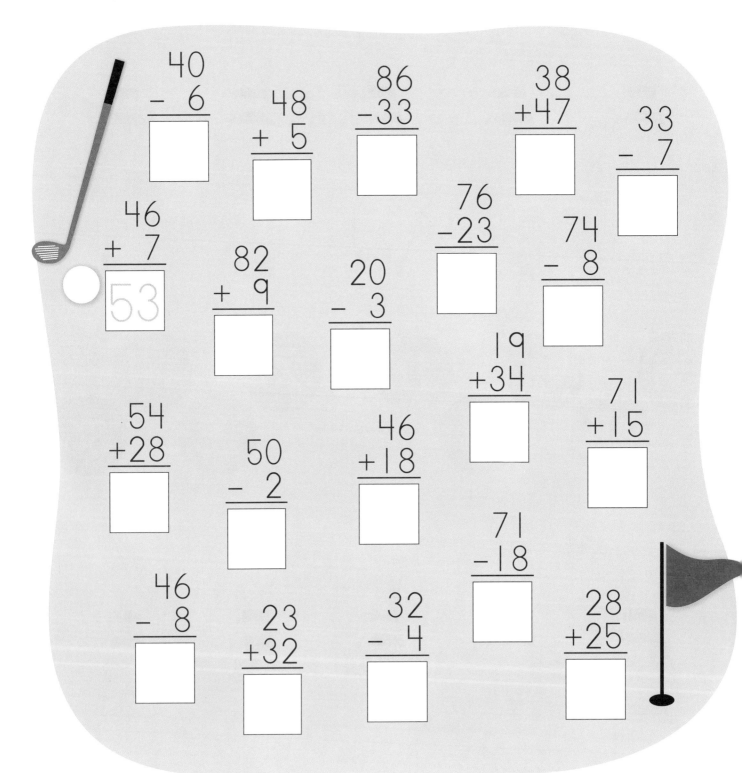

$$\begin{array}{r}40\\-\ 6\\\hline\end{array}$$

$$\begin{array}{r}48\\+\ 5\\\hline\end{array}$$

$$\begin{array}{r}86\\-33\\\hline\end{array}$$

$$\begin{array}{r}38\\+47\\\hline\end{array}$$

$$\begin{array}{r}33\\-\ 7\\\hline\end{array}$$

$$\begin{array}{r}46\\+\ 7\\\hline\end{array}$$ 53

$$\begin{array}{r}82\\+\ 9\\\hline\end{array}$$

$$\begin{array}{r}20\\-\ 3\\\hline\end{array}$$

$$\begin{array}{r}76\\-23\\\hline\end{array}$$

$$\begin{array}{r}74\\-\ 8\\\hline\end{array}$$

$$\begin{array}{r}19\\+34\\\hline\end{array}$$

$$\begin{array}{r}54\\+28\\\hline\end{array}$$

$$\begin{array}{r}50\\-\ 2\\\hline\end{array}$$

$$\begin{array}{r}46\\+18\\\hline\end{array}$$

$$\begin{array}{r}71\\+15\\\hline\end{array}$$

$$\begin{array}{r}71\\-18\\\hline\end{array}$$

$$\begin{array}{r}46\\-\ 8\\\hline\end{array}$$

$$\begin{array}{r}23\\+32\\\hline\end{array}$$

$$\begin{array}{r}32\\-\ 4\\\hline\end{array}$$

$$\begin{array}{r}28\\+25\\\hline\end{array}$$

EMC 4176 • © Evan-Moor Corp.

How Many Points?

▶ Find the answers. Regroup if needed. Then color in the boxes where you had to regroup to see how many points Molly's team got.

23 +46 *69*	75 +19	71 +28	76 −27	65 −34	94 −66	48 −26
99 −63	70 −38	33 +66	64 +28	57 −14	66 −47	54 +35
78 −30	19 +22	42 −32	32 −13	60 −28	37 +36	46 −25
66 −22	96 −48	45 +24	29 −10	68 −21	37 +18	52 +47
99 −66	25 +35	20 +60	38 −21	10 +81	54 +19	44 −23

Molly's team got ☐ points.

Hit the Bull's-Eye

▶ Add up the score for each target.

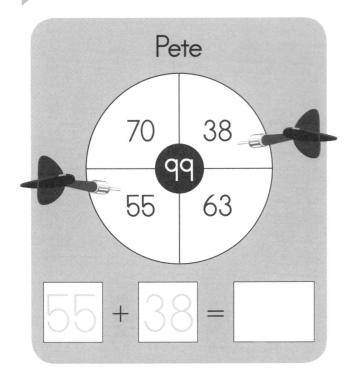

Pete

55 + 38 =

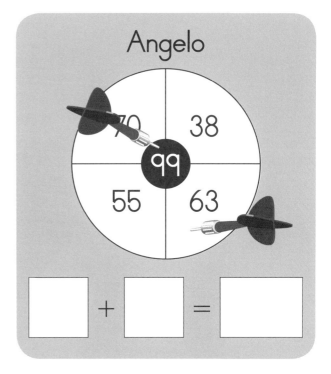

Angelo

☐ + ☐ = ☐

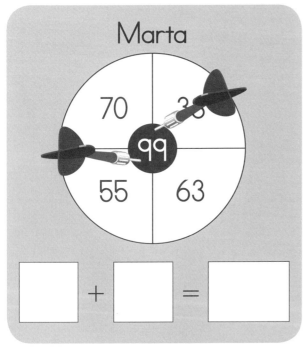

Marta

☐ + ☐ = ☐

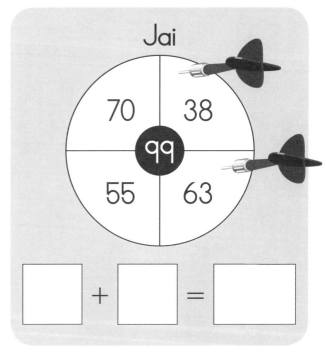

Jai

☐ + ☐ = ☐

Who got the most points?   Pete   Angelo   Marta   Jai

3, 2, 1, Go!

Find the answers to help the runner reach the finish line.

$$\begin{array}{r} 252 \\ +346 \\ \hline 598 \end{array}$$

$$\begin{array}{r} 405 \\ +550 \\ \hline \end{array}$$

$$\begin{array}{r} 721 \\ +\ \ 75 \\ \hline \end{array}$$

$$\begin{array}{r} 488 \\ +410 \\ \hline \end{array}$$

$$\begin{array}{r} 263 \\ +316 \\ \hline \end{array}$$

$$\begin{array}{r} 153 \\ +443 \\ \hline \end{array}$$

$$\begin{array}{r} 105 \\ +382 \\ \hline \end{array}$$

$$\begin{array}{r} 500 \\ +326 \\ \hline \end{array}$$

$$\begin{array}{r} 200 \\ +199 \\ \hline \end{array}$$

$$\begin{array}{r} 624 \\ +134 \\ \hline \end{array}$$

Mystery Letter

▶ Subtract. Color the boxes with **454** as an answer to find the letter on Zack's ball cap.

$$689 - 465$$ $$987 - 533$$ $$857 - 403$$ $$474 - 20$$ $$655 - 324$$
454

$$735 - 123$$ $$958 - 427$$ $$698 - 244$$ $$777 - 453$$ $$687 - 445$$

$$692 - 290$$ $$739 - 315$$ $$576 - 122$$ $$958 - 204$$ $$488 - 233$$

Which letter did you find?

    EMC 4176 • © Evan-Moor Corp.

▶ Add or subtract to get a home run.

796 −465 *331*	655 −324	406 +372	599 −267	252 +346
405 +550	721 +156	488 −408	958 −427	777 −453
105 +382	263 +336	369 −352	687 −445	153 +443
399 −290	200 +199	735 −123	500 +326	947 −627

Regrouping

$$\begin{array}{r} \overset{1}{3}65 \\ +447 \\ \hline 2 \end{array}$$

Add the ones.
Regroup if needed.

$$\begin{array}{r} \overset{1\,1}{3}65 \\ +447 \\ \hline 12 \end{array}$$

Add the tens.
Regroup if needed.

$$\begin{array}{r} \overset{1}{3}65 \\ +447 \\ \hline 812 \end{array}$$

Add the hundreds.

▶ Add.

487 +122	404 +367	795 +105	274 +505
315 +294	777 +123	304 +464	567 +123
456 +261	376 +225	330 +123	642 +188

EMC 4176 • © Evan-Moor Corp.

Regrouping

```
  6 18
  6 7 8
- 2 0 9
───────
        9
```
Subtract the ones.
Regroup if needed.

```
  6 18
  6 7 8
- 2 0 9
───────
      6 9
```
Subtract the tens.
Regroup if needed.

```
  6 18
  6 7 8
- 2 0 9
───────
    4 6 9
```
Subtract the hundreds.

```
  5 1 7
- 2 9 5
───────
        2
```
Subtract the ones.
Regroup if needed.

```
  4 11
  5 1 7
- 2 9 5
───────
      2 2
```
Subtract the tens.
Regroup if needed.

```
  4 11
  5 1 7
- 2 9 5
───────
    2 2 2
```
Subtract the hundreds.

▶ **Subtract.**

```
  483        884        436        635
- 235      - 346      - 164      - 263
─────      ─────      ─────      ─────
```

```
  568        478        851        619
- 174      - 345      - 316      - 295
─────      ─────      ─────      ─────
```

Make a Match

▶ Draw lines to match problems with the same answers. Regroup when needed.

```
  343
 +419
┌──────┐
│      │
└──────┘
```

```
  268
 +503
┌──────┐
│      │
└──────┘
```

```
  609
 +139
┌──────┐
│      │
└──────┘
```

```
  206
 +117
┌──────┐
│      │
└──────┘
```

```
  803
 +167
┌──────┐
│      │
└──────┘
```

```
  534
 +137
┌──────┐
│      │
└──────┘
```

```
  992
 - 22
┌──────┐
│      │
└──────┘
```

```
  880
 -118
┌──────┐
│      │
└──────┘
```

```
  732
 -409
┌──────┐
│      │
└──────┘
```

```
  990
 -319
┌──────┐
│      │
└──────┘
```

```
  980
 -209
┌──────┐
│      │
└──────┘
```

```
  787
 - 39
┌──────┐
│      │
└──────┘
```

EMC 4176 • © Evan-Moor Corp.

Let's Go Shopping!

▶ Shop for sports equipment.
Add or subtract to answer the questions.

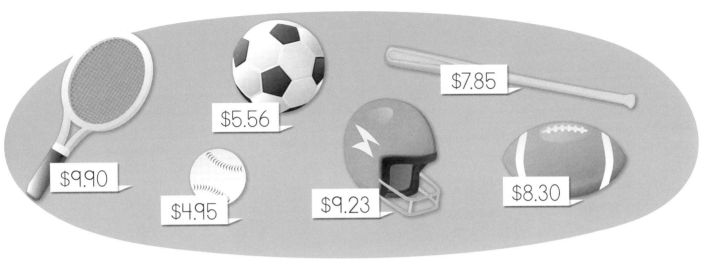

$9.90

$5.56

$4.95

$7.85

$9.23

$8.30

How much are
a baseball and
a bat?

$4.95
+ $7.85
$12.80

How much more
is a tennis racket
than a football?

$.
$.
$.

How much are
a football and
a helmet?

$.
$.
$.

How much more
is a soccer ball
than a baseball?

$.
$.
$.

What two things would you buy?
What would they cost?

$.
$.

_____ and _____ $.

Poor Raul

▶ Raul woke up sick. He must miss the last basketball game. Use the code to find out why Raul must miss the game.

Code
$$125 = H \quad 476 = E \quad 654 = L \quad 350 = A$$
$$555 = S \quad 651 = T \quad 704 = M$$

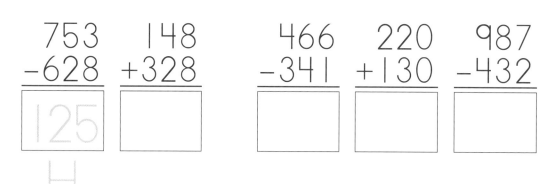

753	148		466	220	987
−628	+328		−341	+130	−432

125

H

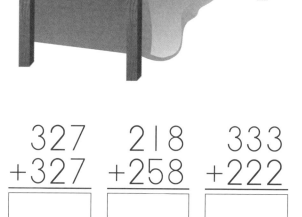

219	104	983
+432	+ 21	−507

940	898	900	764	327	218	333
−236	−422	−550	−209	+327	+258	+222

___ ___ ___ ___ ___ ___ ___

EMC 4176 • © Evan-Moor Corp.

Find the answers. To get a basket, color the boxes with **327** as an answer.

241 + 86 *327*	432 −105	375 − 48	192 + 98	251 −140
329 −132	480 −129	228 + 99	179 +148	742 −453
324 −298	189 +189	340 −189	258 + 69	246 +167
235 −146	579 −185	609 +103	733 −406	100 +227

Archery

Add or subtract to hit the target.

123 +456 579	484 -264	827 +122	992 -820	448 +321
209 -108	681 +210	348 -248	737 +241	654 -543
946 -623	516 -212	242 +215	450 +330	746 -221
489 +210	968 -352	109 +190	207 -104	726 +131

EMC 4176 • © Evan-Moor Corp.

What Am I?

Connect the dots from **50** to **100** to find the creepy creature.

I am a _____.

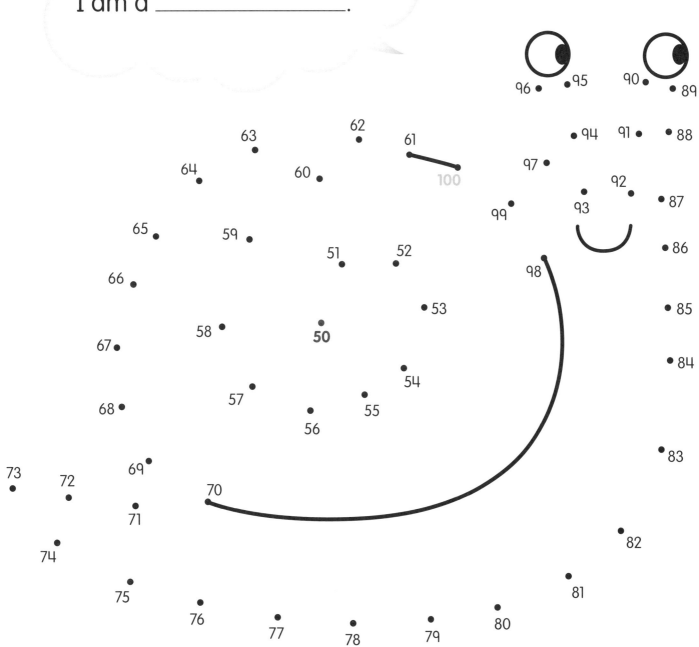

What Is the Missing Number?

▶ Write the missing numbers on the lines.

In Between	After	Before
50 _51_ 52	37 _38_	_66_ 67
26 ___ 28	69 ___	___ 37
82 ___ 84	56 ___	___ 54
37 ___ 39	30 ___	___ 49
29 ___ 31	49 ___	___ 19
42 ___ 44	57 ___	___ 70
39 ___ 41	70 ___	___ 88
68 ___ 70	89 ___	___ 69
59 ___ 61	53 ___	___ 20
92 ___ 94	19 ___	___ 100

EMC 4176 • © Evan-Moor Corp.

Greater Than, Less Than, Equal To

▶ Use one of the symbols in each circle to show which number is more or to show that they are equal.

8 is **greater than** 7	7 is **less than** 8	8 is **equal to** 8
8 $>$ 7	7 $<$ 8	8 $=$ 8

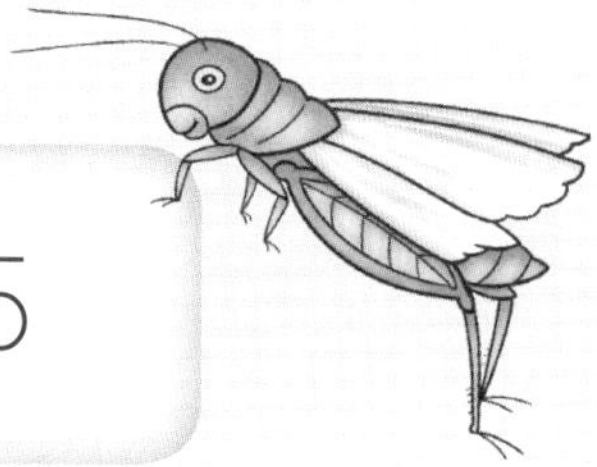

41 $>$ 26

74 $\bigcirc$ 75

15 $\bigcirc$ 10

88 $\bigcirc$ 59

36 $\bigcirc$ 29

65 $\bigcirc$ 95

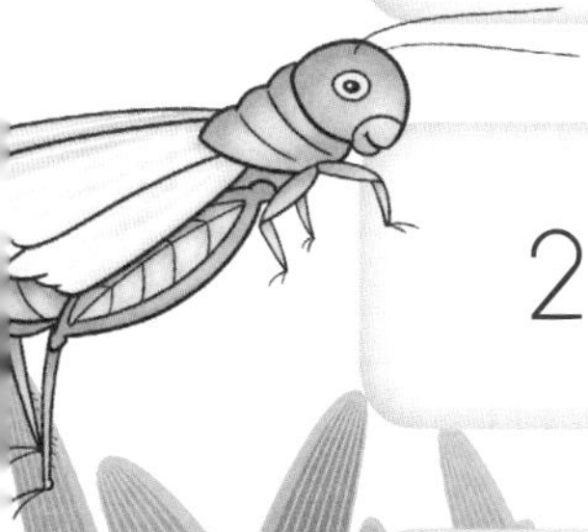

27 $\bigcirc$ 75

46 $\bigcirc$ 46

30 $\bigcirc$ 30

53 $\bigcirc$ 35

50 $\bigcirc$ 37

21 $\bigcirc$ 12

Where Are We Going?

These insects are going home.
Ant will take the **twos** path. Color the twos **green**.
Fly will take the **fives** path. Color the fives **blue**.
Ladybug will take the **tens** path. Color the tens **red**.

2	9	11	25	5	10	18	10	7	23
4	6	8	27	29	15	19	20	9	29
21	25	10	26	25	20	21	30	40	30
23	27	12	14	30	35	40	11	50	60
17	19	18	16	31	32	45	3	75	70
24	33	20	33	60	55	50	45	10	80
29	3	22	3	65	13	25	17	100	90

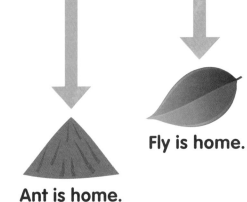

Ant is home.

Fly is home.

Ladybug is home.

EMC 4176 • © Evan-Moor Corp.

Up to 1,000!

▶ Fill in the missing numbers.

100 _101_ _102_ _103_ ____ ____ ____ ____

211 _212_ ____ ____ ____ ____ ____ ____

452 _453_ ____ ____ ____ ____ ____ ____

895 _896_ ____ ____ ____ ____ ____ ____

993 _994_ ____ ____ ____ ____ ____ ____

▶ Fill in the missing numbers.

134 ____ 136	515 ____ 517
301 ____ 303	222 ____ 224
645 ____ 647	715 ____ 717
578 ____ 580	600 ____ 602
499 ____ 501	256 ____ 258

100 to 1,000

▶ Count by **10s**.

100	110	120						
200								
300								
400								
500								
600								
700								
800								
900								
1,000								

▶ Connect the dots.
Count by **10s**.
Start with **200**.

▶ Draw a ladybug
on the leaf.

300
310
330
320
290
280
210
270
220
260
250
230
240

Count the Blocks

▶ Count how many **hundreds**, **tens**, and **ones** there are.
Write how many blocks in all.

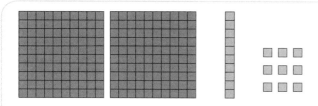

__2__ hundreds + __1__ ten + __9__ ones = __219__

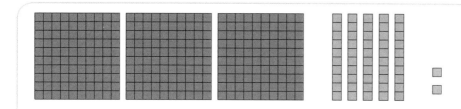

____ hundreds + ____ tens + ____ ones = _____

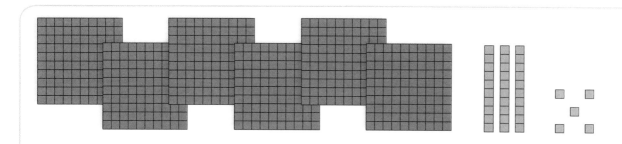

____ hundreds + ____ tens + ____ ones = _____

Hundreds, Tens, Ones

▶ Circle the correct digit in the number.

Circle the hundreds.   ③24

Circle the ones.   289

Circle the hundreds.   462

Circle the tens.   987

Circle the ones.   604

Circle the hundreds.   385

Circle the tens.   913

▶ Write the correct digit.

267   ___ hundreds

785   ___ ones

976   ___ tens

359   ___ ones

704   ___ hundreds

692   ___ tens

481   ___ hundreds

EMC 4176 • © Evan-Moor Corp.

Cross the Pond

▶ Find the answers.
Then color a safe route to the other side.

> **Even** numbers are safe.
>   2, 4, 6, 8, 10, and so on.
>
> **Odd** numbers are crocodiles.
>   1, 3, 5, 7, 9, and so on.

$14 - 8 = 6$

$15 - 8 =$

$6 + 6 =$

$16 - 8 =$

$18 - 9 =$

$7 + 6 =$

$7 + 8 =$

$7 + 5 =$

$14 - 8 =$

$10 - 3 =$

$13 - 5 =$

Fact Families

▶ Make 2 addition problems and 2 subtraction problems for each apple.

8   4   12

$$4 + 8 = 12$$
$$8 + 4 = 12$$
$$12 - 8 = 4$$
$$12 - 4 = 8$$

9   6   15

___ + ___ = ___
___ + ___ = ___
___ − ___ = ___
___ − ___ = ___

5   6   11

___ + ___ = ___
___ + ___ = ___
___ − ___ = ___
___ − ___ = ___

9   8   17

___ + ___ = ___
___ + ___ = ___
___ − ___ = ___
___ − ___ = ___

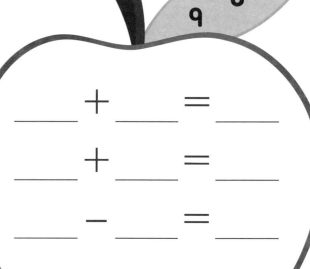

What's Eating My Garden?

▶ Find the answers that have **6** in the ones place.
Write the letters of those problems in order on the blank lines.
Then you will know what's eating my garden.

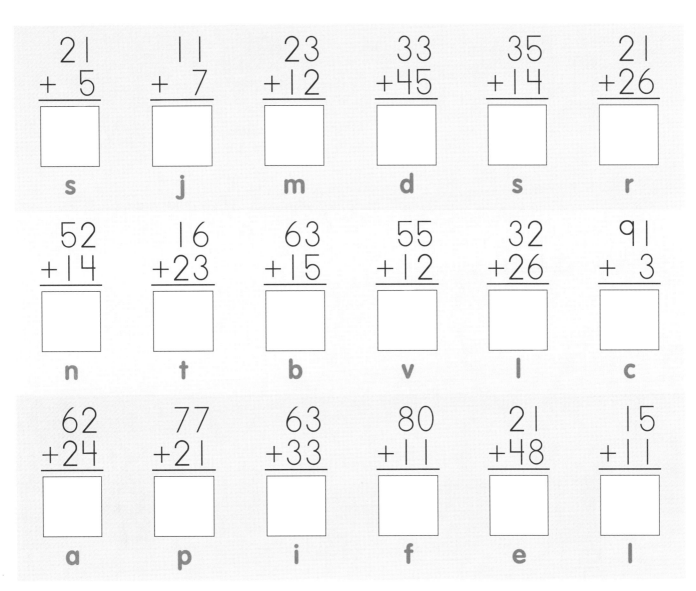

```
  21        11        23        33        35        21
+  5      +  7      + 12      + 45      + 14      + 26
[    ]    [    ]    [    ]    [    ]    [    ]    [    ]
   s         j         m         d         s         r

  52        16        63        55        32        91
+ 14      + 23      + 15      + 12      + 26      +  3
[    ]    [    ]    [    ]    [    ]    [    ]    [    ]
   n         t         b         v         l         c

  62        77        63        80        21        15
+ 24      + 21      + 33      + 11      + 48      + 11
[    ]    [    ]    [    ]    [    ]    [    ]    [    ]
   a         p         i         f         e         l
```

▶ What's eating my garden?

[___ ___ ___ ___ ___]

Name the Critters

▶ Solve the problems. Use the code to name the critters.

129-m	412-g	779-u	303-d
533-a	798-r	339-y	768-w
897-o	378-b	999-l	

$$\begin{array}{r}594\\+405\\\hline 999\end{array}\quad\begin{array}{r}433\\+100\\\hline\end{array}\quad\begin{array}{r}828\\-525\\\hline\end{array}\quad\begin{array}{r}126\\+213\\\hline\end{array}\quad\begin{array}{r}226\\+152\\\hline\end{array}\quad\begin{array}{r}274\\+505\\\hline\end{array}\quad\begin{array}{r}879\\-467\\\hline\end{array}$$

l ___ ___ ___ ___ ___ ___

$$\begin{array}{r}999\\-231\\\hline\end{array}\quad\begin{array}{r}684\\+213\\\hline\end{array}\quad\begin{array}{r}653\\+145\\\hline\end{array}\quad\begin{array}{r}659\\-530\\\hline\end{array}$$

___ ___ ___ ___

Beehives

```
  38
+20
----
  58
```

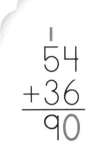

```
¹
  54
+36
----
  90
```

```
¹
  18
+53
----
  71
```

▶ Find the answers. Regroup if you need to.

```
¹
  38
+54
----
  92
```

```
  21
+46
----
```

```
  23
+48
----
```

```
  36
+42
----
```

```
  87
+ 5
----
```

```
  52
+35
----
```

```
  19
+26
----
```

```
  18
+31
----
```

```
  46
+26
----
```

```
  76
+23
----
```

```
  25
+18
----
```

```
  62
+34
----
```

```
  77
+ 6
----
```

```
  24
+56
----
```

```
  45
+23
----
```

Butterflies

$$\overset{1}{6}7$$
$$+29$$
$$\overline{96}$$

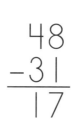

$$48$$
$$-31$$
$$\overline{17}$$

$$\overset{2}{\cancel{3}}\overset{18}{\cancel{8}}$$
$$-19$$
$$\overline{19}$$

▶ Find the answers. Regroup if you need to.

$$\overset{1}{5}8$$
$$+29$$
$$\boxed{87}$$

$$75$$
$$-19$$
$$\boxed{}$$

$$24$$
$$+36$$
$$\boxed{}$$

$$49$$
$$+29$$
$$\boxed{}$$

$$25$$
$$+28$$
$$\boxed{}$$

$$73$$
$$-16$$
$$\boxed{}$$

$$72$$
$$+17$$
$$\boxed{}$$

$$26$$
$$-14$$
$$\boxed{}$$

$$60$$
$$-22$$
$$\boxed{}$$

$$42$$
$$+39$$
$$\boxed{}$$

$$33$$
$$+49$$
$$\boxed{}$$

$$85$$
$$-48$$
$$\boxed{}$$

$$77$$
$$-31$$
$$\boxed{}$$

$$39$$
$$+27$$
$$\boxed{}$$

$$71$$
$$-38$$
$$\boxed{}$$

EMC 4176 • © Evan-Moor Corp.

How Many Legs?

▶ Count the legs to find out how many.

How many ants? ___1___

How many legs on each ant? ___6___

How many legs in all? ___6___

How many frogs? _____

How many legs on each frog? _____

How many legs in all? _____

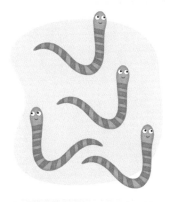

How many worms? _____

How many legs on each worm? _____

How many legs in all? _____

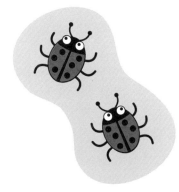

How many ladybugs? _____

How many legs on each ladybug? _____

How many legs in all? _____

Twos, Fives

▶ Count by **2s**. Then solve the problems.

0 2 __4__ ____ ____ ____ ____ ____

3	2	8	0	5
×2	×2	×2	×2	×2
☐	☐	☐	☐	☐

4	1	6	7	9
×2	×2	×2	×2	×2
☐	☐	☐	☐	☐

▶ Count by **5s**. Then solve the problems.

0 5 __10__ ____ ____ ____ ____ ____

5	2	9	3	7
×5	×5	×5	×5	×5
☐	☐	☐	☐	☐

0	4	8	1	6
×5	×5	×5	×5	×5
☐	☐	☐	☐	☐

EMC 4176 • © Evan-Moor Corp.

Name the Creatures

Multiply. Use the code to name the creatures.

2-a	6-n	14-s	3-g	25-w
8-e	16-i	4-b	9-l	12-o
20-t	5-r	10-f		

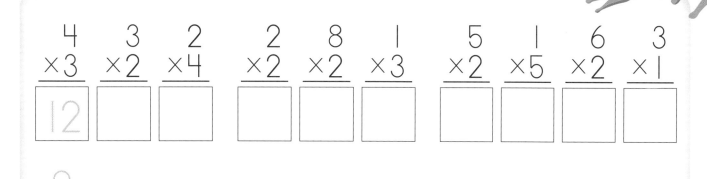

4
×3
= 12   o

3
×2

2
×4

2
×2

8
×2

1
×3

5
×2

1
×5

6
×2

3
×1

____ ____ ____   ____ ____ ____   ____ ____ ____ ____

4
×5

5
×5

3
×4

2
×7

6
×1

1
×2

2
×8

3
×3

7
×2

____ ____ ____   ____ ____ ____   ____ ____ ____

A Multiplication Table

▶ Write the missing numbers.

X	2	5	10
1	2		
2	4		
3			
4		20	
5			
6			60
7	14	35	
8			
9			90

Telling Time

▶ Count by **5s** around the clock.
From one number to the next is five minutes.

▶ What time is it?

_____:_____   _____:_____   _____:_____   _____:_____

Snail Race

▶ Read the clocks to see how long it took each snail to finish the race.

	Started	Finished	
			_____ hour
			_____ hours
			_____ hours
			_____ hours

▶ Circle the fastest snail.
How long did the snail take? _____

Use the code to solve the riddle.

We fly and we buzz.
We have black and yellow fuzz.
In a hive in a tree,
A bunch of us will be.

Code

5:45-s	10:30-h
6:45-b	9:15-o
8:30-e	4:15-n
11:45-y	

Read each clock. On the line, write the time it will be in one hour. Then write the matching letter in the box.

Time

in one hour 10:30

Time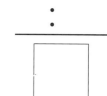

in one hour

What are we?
Circle the picture.

 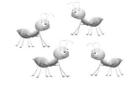 

How Much Money Do I Have?

▶ Count the money to see which creature has the most money.

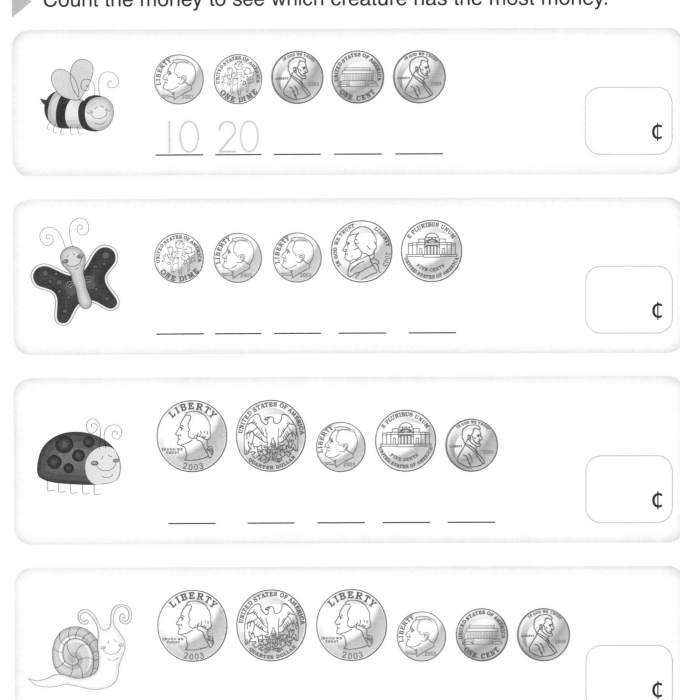

10 20 ___ ___ ___   ⊂ [ ] ¢

___ ___ ___ ___ ___   ⊂ [ ] ¢

___ ___ ___ ___ ___   ⊂ [ ] ¢

___ ___ ___ ___ ___ ___   ⊂ [ ] ¢

Who has the most money? _____

EMC 4176 • © Evan-Moor Corp.

Make a Surprise

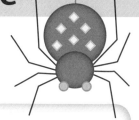

▶ Use the shapes to make an object.
Then tell how much your object costs.

1¢   5¢   10¢   25¢ $1.00

I made a _____.

It would cost $_____._____.

Shopping

> Count the money to see how much each toy cost.

Millie bought a balloon.
How much did it cost?

$_____._____

Kim bought a toy butterfly.
How much did it cost?

$_____._____

George bought a toy truck.
How much did it cost?

$_____._____

Anthony bought a toy ladybug.
How much did it cost?

$_____._____

EMC 4176 • © Evan-Moor Corp.

Shapes

▶ Draw the things listed below using only these shapes.

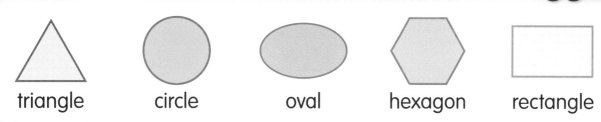

triangle   circle   oval   hexagon   rectangle

ladybug

snail

ant

butterfly

Name the Shapes

▶ Mark the sides with a **red** crayon. Put an **X** on each corner. Write the name of each shape and how many sides and corners it has.

square	circle
hexagon	triangle
rectangle	pentagon

name ___square___

sides __4__   corners __4__

name _____

sides _____   corners _____

name _____

sides _____   corners _____

name _____

sides _____   corners _____

name _____

sides _____   corners _____

name _____

sides _____   corners _____

EMC 4176 • © Evan-Moor Corp.

▶ Match the shapes to the names.

sphere

rectangular prism

pyramid

cone

cube

cylinder

Ants Ate My Cookies

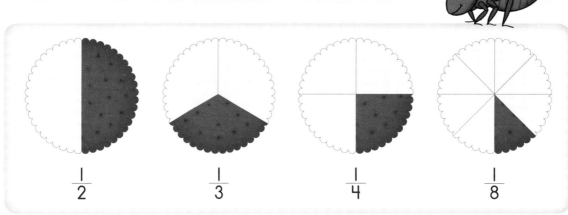

▶ Color to show the fractions.

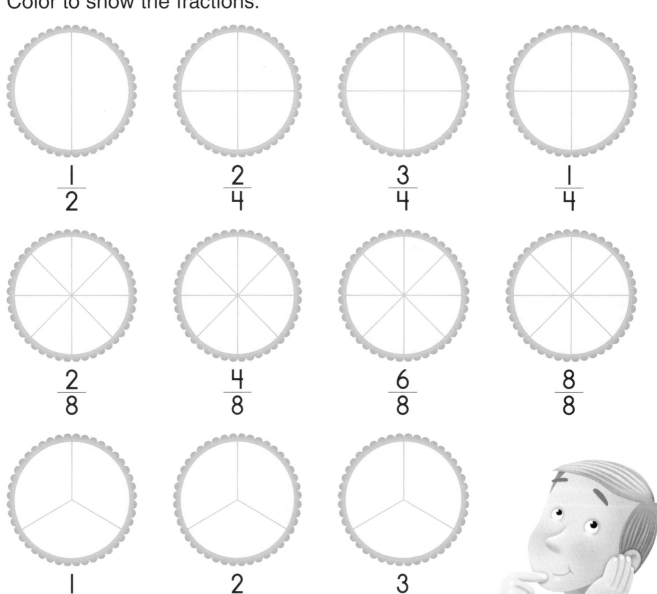

EMC 4176 • © Evan-Moor Corp.

▶ Color the ladybugs.

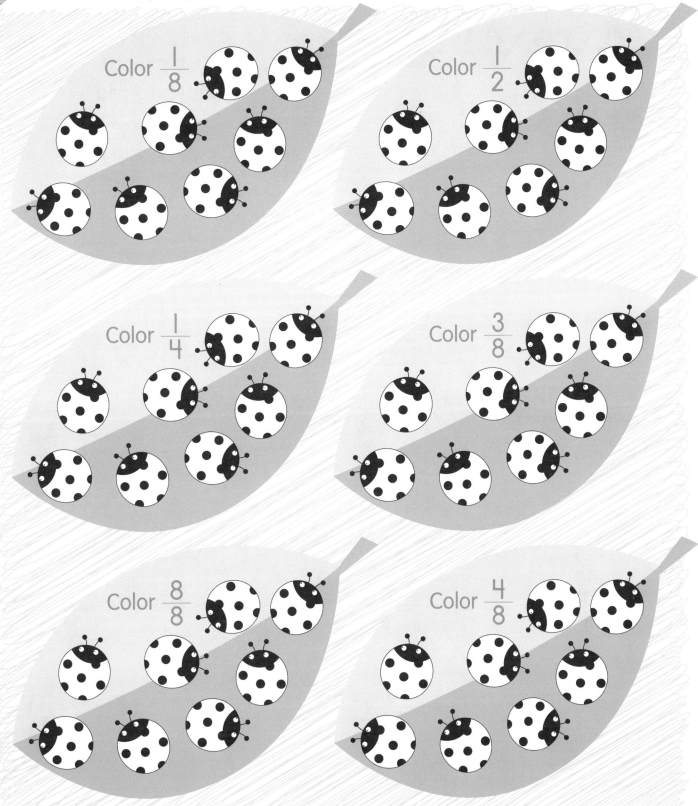

Color $\frac{1}{8}$

Color $\frac{1}{2}$

Color $\frac{1}{4}$

Color $\frac{3}{8}$

Color $\frac{8}{8}$

Color $\frac{4}{8}$

How Many?

▶ Color one part of the graph for each creepy critter.

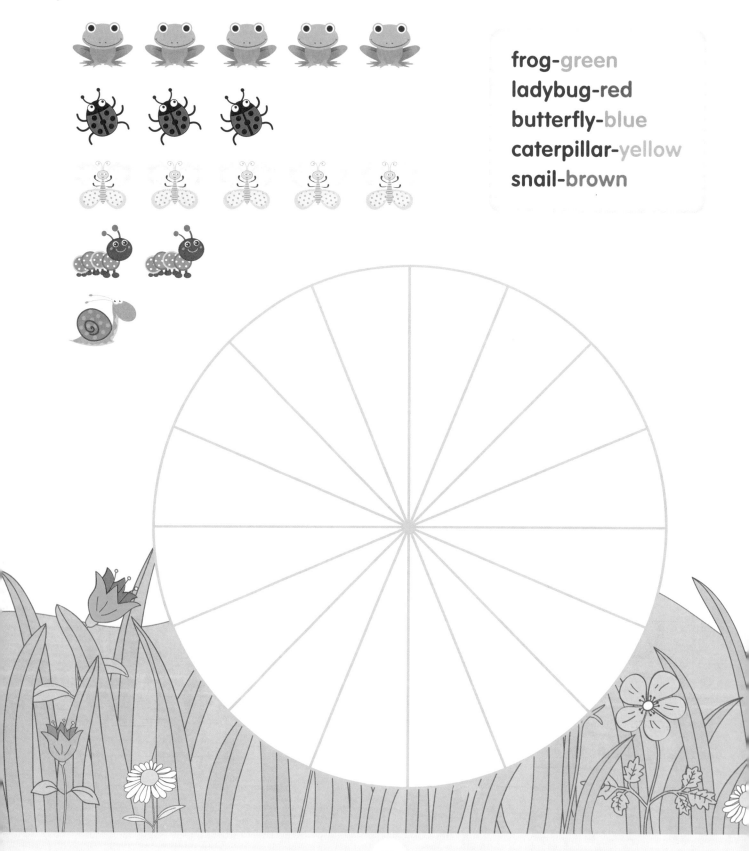

frog-green
ladybug-red
butterfly-blue
caterpillar-yellow
snail-brown

Find the answers to reach the planet.

$$\begin{array}{r} 6 \\ +7 \\ \hline \end{array} \qquad \begin{array}{r} 5 \\ +6 \\ \hline \end{array} \qquad \begin{array}{r} 4 \\ +7 \\ \hline \end{array} \qquad \begin{array}{r} 9 \\ +5 \\ \hline \end{array} \qquad \begin{array}{r} 7 \\ +5 \\ \hline \end{array}$$

$$\begin{array}{r} 9 \\ +3 \\ \hline \end{array} \qquad \begin{array}{r} 9 \\ +6 \\ \hline \end{array} \qquad \begin{array}{r} 8 \\ +8 \\ \hline \end{array} \qquad \begin{array}{r} 8 \\ +4 \\ \hline \end{array} \qquad \begin{array}{r} 4 \\ +8 \\ \hline \end{array}$$

$$\begin{array}{r} 8 \\ +5 \\ \hline \end{array} \qquad \begin{array}{r} 9 \\ +9 \\ \hline \end{array} \qquad \begin{array}{r} 2 \\ +8 \\ \hline \end{array} \qquad \begin{array}{r} 8 \\ +3 \\ \hline \end{array} \qquad \begin{array}{r} 7 \\ +7 \\ \hline \end{array}$$

$$\begin{array}{r} 9 \\ +7 \\ \hline \end{array} \qquad \begin{array}{r} 6 \\ +6 \\ \hline \end{array} \qquad \begin{array}{r} 6 \\ +5 \\ \hline \end{array} \qquad \begin{array}{r} 9 \\ +4 \\ \hline \end{array} \qquad \begin{array}{r} 8 \\ +7 \\ \hline \end{array}$$

Mystery Picture

▶ Count by **10s** to connect the dots. Then color the picture.

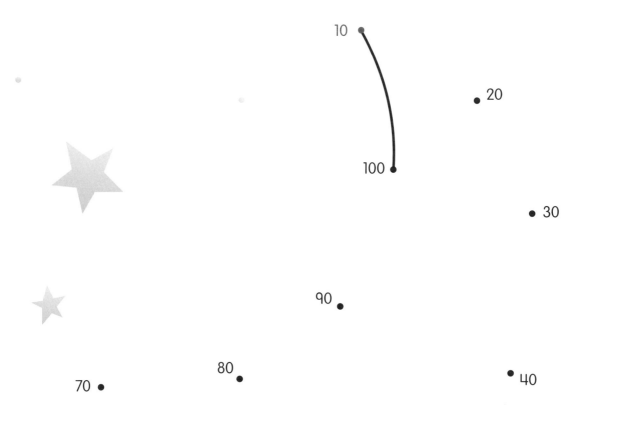

10

20

100

30

90

80   40

70

60   50

▶ Fill in the missing numbers.

10			40	
	80			

EMC 4176 • © Evan-Moor Corp.

Race to the Moon

Fill in the missing numbers to see which ship reaches the moon first. The winner ends with the highest number.

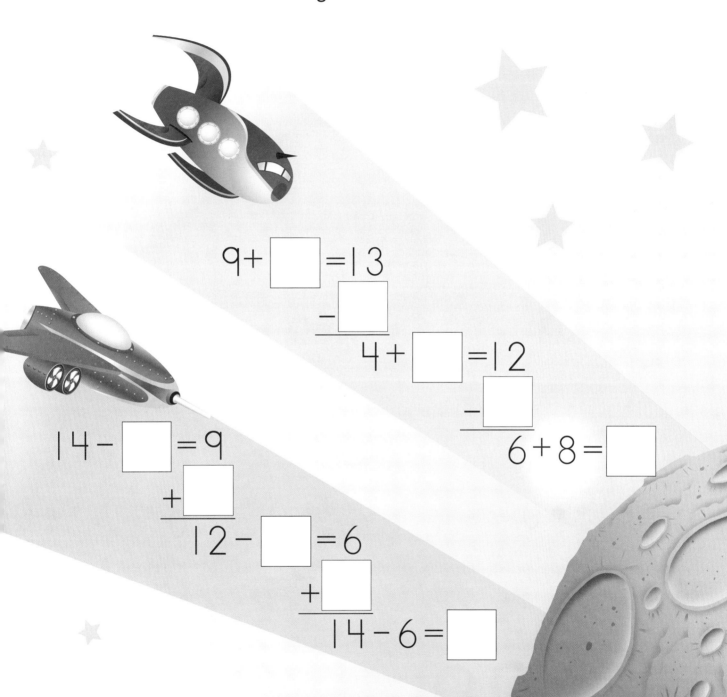

$$9 + \boxed{} = 13$$
$$-\boxed{}$$

$$4 + \boxed{} = 12$$
$$-\boxed{}$$
$$6 + 8 = \boxed{}$$

$$14 - \boxed{} = 9$$
$$+\boxed{}$$
$$12 - \boxed{} = 6$$
$$+\boxed{}$$
$$14 - 6 = \boxed{}$$

Circle the winner.

Robots

▶ Add the number at the top of each robot.

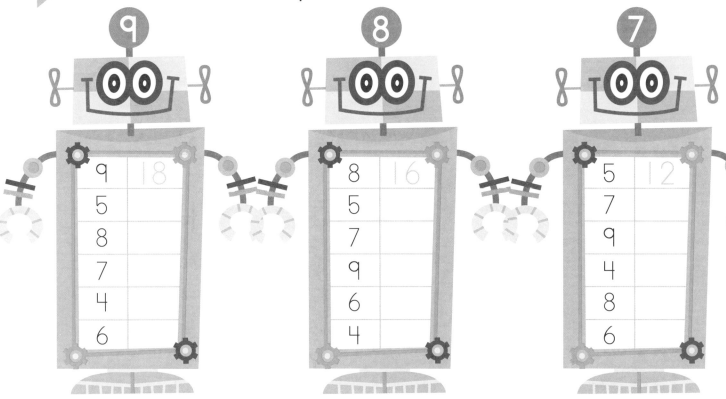

9	18
5	
8	
7	
4	
6	

8	16
5	
7	
9	
6	
4	

5	12
7	
9	
4	
8	
6	

▶ Subtract the number at the top of each robot.

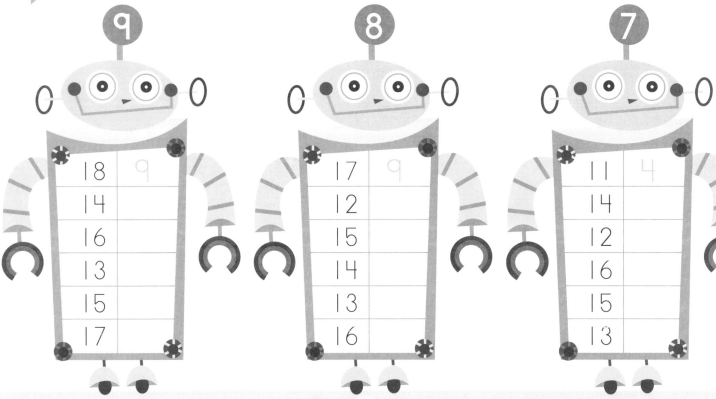

18	9
14	
16	
13	
15	
17	

17	9
12	
15	
14	
13	
16	

11	4
14	
12	
16	
15	
13	

Number Names

▶ Write the number names in the boxes on the crossword puzzle.

one   four   seven
two   five   eight
three   six   twelve

Across

1. 5
2. 2
4. 3
5. 7
6. 8

Down

1. 4
3. 1
4. 12
5. 6

Counting by 5s

▶ Count by **5s**.
Color the boxes **red**.

1	2	3	4	5	6	7	8	9	10
11	12	13	14	15	16	17	18	19	20
21	22	23	24	25	26	27	28	29	30
31	32	33	34	35	36	37	38	39	40
41	42	43	44	45	46	47	48	49	50
51	52	53	54	55	56	57	58	59	60
61	62	63	64	65	66	67	68	69	70
71	72	73	74	75	76	77	78	79	80
81	82	83	84	85	86	87	88	89	90
91	92	93	94	95	96	97	98	99	100

▶ Fill in the missing numbers.

5	10			25			
	60				80		

EMC 4176 • © Evan-Moor Corp.